The A to ... nt Tools

First published 2012

www.trainingforvas.com

ISBN-13: 978-1470177515

ISBN-10: 147017751X

Copyright © Helen Stothard

The moral right of Helen Stothard to be identified as the author of this work has been asserted by her in accordance with the Copyright, Designs and Patents Act 1988.

All rights reserved. No part of this publication may be reproduced, stored or transmitted in any form, or by any means, electronic, mechanical or photocopying, recording or otherwise, without express written permission of the author.

Limit of Liability/Disclaimer of Warranty: This book is designed to provide information about the subject matter. It is sold with the understanding that the publisher and authors are not engaged in rendering legal, coaching or other professional services. While the publisher and author have used their best efforts in preparing this book, they make no representations or warranties with respect to the accuracy or completeness of the contents of this book and specifically disclaim any implied warranties of merchantability or fitness for a particular purpose. No warranty may be created or extended by sales representatives or written sales materials. This book is not intended or should be a substitute for therapy or professional advice. The views and opinions expressed in this page are strictly those of the author. The advice and strategies contained herein may not be suitable for your situation. The publisher is not engaged in rendering professional services, and you should consult a competent professional where appropriate. Neither the publisher nor author shall be liable for any loss of profit or any other commercial damages, including but not limited to special, incidental, consequential, or other damages. This document is provided for educational purposes only. The reader assumes all risk and responsibility for the usage of any information or ideas contained in this guide. If you do not wish to be bound by the above, you may return the book to the publisher for a full refund.

Contents

Introduction 5
Praise for the A to Z of Virtual Assistant Tools 6
Amazon 7
Artisteer 8
Audacity 9
Blogging 10
Bookkeeping 11
Buffer 12
Capsule 14
Collaboration 16
Cloud Computing 17
ColorPic 18
Domain Name 19
Dreamstime 21
Dropbox 22
Eventbrite 23
Evernote 24
Express Scribe 26
Facebook 27
Feedly 29
FreeIndex 30
GetClicky 31
Google Apps 32
Health 34
Hootsuite 36
iPad and iPhone 38
Information Commissioner's Office 39
Jing 40
JotForm 41
Kindle 42
Klout 43
LinkedIn 44
MailChimp 46
MinuteDock 48
Mirror.me 50
Nefsis 51

- Networking 52
- Office Space 53
- Payroo 54
- PhotoSync 55
- Pixlr 56
- PrimoPDF 57
- QR Codes 58
- Rapportive 59
- SAYNOTO0870.com 60
- Skype 61
- SVA – Society of Virtual Assistants 63
- Trainingforvas.com 64
- Twitter 65
- Unlimited Data - mobile 67
- Video 69
- VoIP 70
- WordPress 72
- Xero 73
- YouTube 75
- Zemanta 76
- About Helen Stothard 77
- Contact Helen Stothard 78

Introduction

The A to Z of Virtual Assistant Tools is a directory of some of the tools that I use in the day to day running of my Virtual Assistant (VA) business. These are the tools that save me time, make me more efficient for my clients and help me run my business more smoothly.

This book is designed to help Virtual Assistants at all stages of their career; for those who are just starting out I hope this will give some idea of the resources available to assist in your future ventures, and for those who have been working as a Virtual Assistant for a while, I hope these tools will help you streamline both your client and business tasks, to save time in all aspects of your organisation.

The Virtual Assistant Tools in this book range from information for you to consider during the set-up process, to online resources to assist you with the running of your business. Furthermore, most of them are free, or offer a trial version, so you can try them and experience how they can work for you.

As you can imagine, there are many more resources available than are listed in this book. In the A to Z of Virtual Assistant Tools, I've listed the ones that are my favourites; I love to use them and they have had the biggest positive impact on my business.

Enjoy!

Helen

Praise for the A to Z of Virtual Assistant Tools

*"As a new VA just starting out (my website only launched earlier this month!), **The A-Z of Virtual Assistant Tools** is a great book! It's opened my eyes to a great deal of tools and resources that I'd never heard of. I will be trying out a lot of them to see how they can assist me in my new VA business and hopefully this will prevent me needing to take time out to streamline my own tasks in the future!"*

Tracey A Dixon, Virtual Assistant

"I'm not a VA and learned more from reading this book than from any 'Greatest Top Ten' lists! With resources to help streamline your business, reach new customers, save time and make more money, this would be ideal for any business owner, VA or not!"

Nikki Pilkington, Social Media Marketing Support

"I purchased this book and didn't think that I would get much out of it being that I am based in NZ but I read and it is just brilliant! All the tips and tricks I have now integrated into my own business and would definitely recommend to any VA needing some guidance on the technology out there - then this book is a great tool for you!"

Carole Unkovich, Virtual Assistant

Amazon

Don't underestimate Amazon as a business tool. It can help your business in several ways. It's not just somewhere to look at when you're buying presents.

As a northern lass I have an eye for a bargain and shop around for my stationery. I often find that Amazon are the cheapest when it comes to buying ink for my printer, memory and hard drives for my laptop and other business gadgets like my portable scanner.

Add to this that they have an affiliate scheme so you can actually have your own Amazon store on your website and you can't go wrong. Sarah Bradley over at Help Ahoy has integrated her Amazon store into her website http://www.helpahoy.com/ and every time one of us buys something via her store she earns a few pence. Granted it's not going to make you a millionaire but every little helps.

http://www.amazon.co.uk

Artisteer

Artisteer is a WYSIWYG theme designer that can be used for html sites and WordPress. The software isn't free but you can download a free trial to see if it suits you. It's perfect if you are struggling to find a WordPress theme that fits both your colours and layout requirements. The theme has plenty of options that can be edited by the end user, and once purchased you can download updates of the software for up to a year.

If you are stuck for ideas then the theme generator will either provide a full theme, or simply make suggestions for a header or background. There are various editing options available, including textures, transparency and sheet size which make this a really useful tool to have in your VA arsenal.

The beauty of Artisteer is that it allows you to have widgets in the header, footer and side bar and it gives you a lot more flexibility than some of the free themes that are out there.

The exclusive intelligentVA Members theme shown below was created in Artisteer. The screen shot shows the Artisteer software.

http://www.artisteer.com/

Audacity

Audacity is a free cross platform sound editor. It's a great tool to record audio to accompany your presentations.

Audacity allows you to record sound clips, and re-record them if they aren't quite right. Imagine trying to record an hour of audio and messing up in the last five minutes. Break it down instead into smaller sound bites and you only have to record a few minutes audio if you make a mistake.

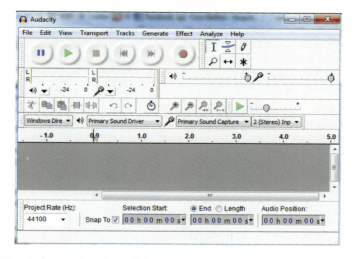

To start recording just click the red button, then click it again to stop. You can then use the menu to save the file in a variety of formats. If you need to jump to a specific section of the recording use the selection start and end/length options as well.

http://audacity.sourceforge.net/

Blogging

Blogging is one of the easiest things you can do to attract visitors to your website, and it doesn't cost you anything other than your time.

There are several blogging platforms available, although you will see later on in this book that my favourite is WordPress (self hosted).

Blogging is a way of sharing your knowledge and expertise with potential clients. Show them what you know, and share information with them.

A blog is personal, no two blogs are the same, but remember to write in the appropriate tone. I wouldn't use the same language in my running blog as I would in my business blog. One would be more light hearted and personal than the other.

Use images to enhance your blog post, always ensuring that you have the appropriate copyright. Invite others to guest post on your blog, then guest post on other blogs to build your reputation.

There are a lot of people willing to help you learn how to blog, I would recommend reading Nikki Pilkington's 30 Day Blogging Challenge or her 299 Steps to Blogging Heaven guide. I found them very useful.

http://www.nikkipilkington.com

Bookkeeping

Bookkeeping is essential to keep track of the success of your business, and to keep records in order to complete your tax return. Our resident bookkeeping expert Nicola Wilson, from Totally4Business, regularly keeps us up to date on the intelligentVA website about the easiest ways to keep records, and is also our resident Xero trainer as well. (we cover Xero in more detail later in this guide)

Bookkeeping can be done on a spreadsheet if you wish but we prefer to use the cloud based system Xero as this gives much more information at your fingertips. Set up automated invoices, have a bank statement or credit card statement import directly into your accounts and see at a glance the balance sheet, debtors and creditors or a profit and loss statement, all information which a spreadsheet system would struggle to provide as quickly or possibly as accurately.

It's a good idea to maintain a separate bank account, credit card and PayPal account for your business as this makes it easier to keep track of your transactions.

We have a resident tax expert on the intelligentVA website, Steve Knowles, from Knowles Warwick. Steve offers guidance on topics such as Self Assessment, Money Laundering, the Bribery Act and other similar areas that will affect your Virtual Assistant business.

One thing to remember about bookkeeping is that if you offer it as a service to your clients then you must be regulated under the Money Laundering Regulations. This can either be with a professional bookkeeping body or via the HMRC themselves. This applies whether you are outsourcing the work or carrying it out yourself.

http://www.totally4business.co.uk

http://www.knowleswarwick.com

http://www.xero.com

http://www.hmrc.gov.uk/MLR/

Buffer

Have you ever come across a great article on a website that you wanted to share on Twitter but didn't want to post just yet? Would you like to post your tweets throughout the day? Buffer is a great app for scheduling tweets and spreading them out so that they don't all appear within a few minutes of each other.

You can choose which days your tweets will appear, so no need to worry about boring people with business tweets on a weekend either. You can even specify what time of day these tweets go out.

Set aside ten minutes on a morning to find suitable content, then add it to Buffer enabling it to appear over the rest of the day or week. This doesn't overload your followers timelines. I would certainly recommend this to some newspaper and news channel twitter accounts who are silent for hours then bombard me with several tweets in the space of five minutes.

Using the browser add-ons that are available in Firefox, Chrome or Safari means you can click on the Buffer icon and compose a tweet containing your message and the relevant website link in seconds. There's an app for Android and iPhone, or the option to email to your Buffer as well.

The free account allows up to 10 tweets to be stored in your Buffer account at any one time, 1 Twitter account and 1 Facebook account. If this isn't enough to meet your requirements then paid plans start from just $10 a month and allow a lot more options, including a larger tweet count, more social accounts and team members.

The analytics show you how many clicks your tweet received and the reach that each message achieved.

Once you have added content to your Buffer you can re-order them to ensure that the messages go out at the most appropriate time.

Buffer kindly sends you a polite email reminder when you need to add in more content so you don't run dry!

http://bufferapp.com

Capsule

Capsule is a cloud-based customer relationship management (CRM) system that will allow you to integrate your accounts, newsletter and website contact form in one place.

Contacts
You can import your existing contacts via .csv spreadsheet, .vcf file, from LinkedIn or Outlook. It's a good idea before you do this to really think about what you want to get out of the system once it's up and running. Add tags or notes at this stage, it saves you a lot of time on updates later on.

Cases
You can use cases to manage specific projects or events. This creates an area where you can bring different contacts together, for example, a client who is a builder creates a case for each building project. We link this to the client, then add contacts such as the plumber, carpenter and plasterer. This way if we have a query relating to the project we know exactly who was working on it, and can have notes and tasks related to the project in one place. We can then view this case from any of the relevant contact records. We have also used cases for event management to monitor who attended events. You can send one email to everyone involved in the case, so this is a great time saver.

Opportunities
This is used to manage your sales pipeline. You can keep an eye on the proposals that you have submitted, track the likelihood of the proposal being accepted and also assign tasks to a particular opportunity.

Email Dropbox
Using the email dropbox function you can copy all your emails into the contact record, be they incoming or outgoing. You can set up your email client with a forwarding rule so that all incoming mail goes into your database but take care that all your personal mail doesn't end up in there as well.

For Google Apps users there is a contextual gadget add in which makes it even easier to create or update contacts from your Google Mail inbox.

Tasks
You can choose to receive a daily reminder of your tasks in your email inbox. If you wish you can assign tasks to a contact or just set a personal reminder, and you can view your outstanding tasks on the task calendar as well as from within the contact record.

Mobile
There is a mobile phone application which is accessible via any mobile phone with a web browser. This allows you to view contact information, history, make calls and send emails, you will also be able to add, snooze or complete tasks whilst out and about.

Integration
Capsule allows integration with other tools such as Xero, MailChimp and your website contact form. All of which reduces the amount of data entry and duplication. There are several other add ons or integrations available.

Free Trial
It's simple user interface makes it easy to learn, and you can sign up for a free trial.

http://www.capsulecrm.com

Collaboration

This is one of the most important tools on your Virtual Assistant journey, and the best thing is its free. It can be very lonely setting up your own business, particularly if you've come from a bustling office environment. The way to combat this is to collaborate with other Virtual Assistants.

The VA industry is stronger for collaborating rather than competing against itself.

What we find at our intelligentVA coffee mornings is a mix of experience; VAs just starting out on their journey chatting to VAs who have been in the business for several years. We all have different skill sets, we often work in different markets, some purely virtual, some working from clients offices, and others a mix of the two.

Yet what we offer each other is that shared knowledge and experience. Sometimes you can be too close to a problem to see the solution, yet chatting it over while having a coffee often leads to ideas you hadn't considered. We see it at every meeting.

It's not just about sharing knowledge though, sometimes it's nice to know that you have someone to listen, who understands what you are going through, has perhaps been through it themselves.

Collaboration can be online through groups like our intelligentVA Facebook group or LinkedIn group, through informal meet ups like our coffee mornings or more formal sessions like our learning days.

Seek out others in your industry, get to know them, build a relationship and your business will be all the stronger for it.

http://www.facebook.com/groups/intelligentva

http://www.linkedin.com/groups/intelligentVA-3906866

Cloud Computing

Throughout this book you will hear me talk about cloud software and cloud computing. But what are they?

I tried to find a non technical definition for you but they were all very wordy, so here is my attempt:

"Cloud Computing is a service that is available over an internet connection as opposed to purchasing a product that can only be accessed from the machine on which it is installed."

If you go to PC World and buy Office 2007 on a disc, bring it home and install it on your computer you have installed a 'product'. If you log onto a website and use Facebook using your user name and password you are using a 'service'.

Cloud services are not dependent on any particular machine, and this is one of the reasons that we like them so much. You can work from any compatible computer, Smartphone or tablet with an internet connection. The data is not stored on your device but in the 'cloud' - the service providers own data centre, often meaning it is backed up for you as well.

If you are able to access the cloud you are no longer tied to a static workplace. You can work from your local coffee shop, hotel lounge or even a clients office subject to an internet connection.

The ash cloud that grounded thousands of flights the other year would not have stopped my business working, so long as I was able to access a computer with an internet connection as I could still access my emails, my client files and the relevant cloud services I needed to carry out my work.

There are many examples of cloud services throughout this guide because they make your business more efficient.

ColorPic

This is a handy little free tool for anyone working with websites or graphics. Not sure of the correct colour 'name'? Then open up ColorPic and hover over the colour you are trying to identify.

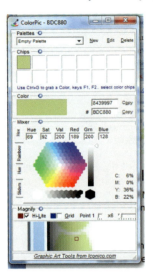

As you move your cursor the colour is identified in the 'Color' box and you get the hex code #, RGB and CMYB values. It displays web safe colours and names as well.

This is helpful if you are trying to match a project to a clients existing website or documentation but don't have access to the designers brand pack.

The ColorPic has a magnifier included to help you grab the colour from a high resolution monitor.

http://www.iconico.com/colorpic/

Domain Name

When you first set up your VA business you need to get your domain name purchased, even if you're not yet ready to set up your website you will need it so that you have a professional email address.

Some companies will offer you a free domain name when you purchase your hosting, this is great, but do check and make sure you will be the owner of the domain if you choose to leave them later.

I have used 123-Reg for a long time to purchase my domain names, some are just parked there ready for the day I wish to use them, some are used solely with Google Apps for email and others are redirected to my hosting space and used on my websites.

Look for a company that offers easy access to manage your domains and that also offers a competitive price.

Of course the hardest part is choosing the right domain name! Let's not dwell on how long I have spent in the past pondering over possible options or realising that the name I most wanted was already gone. Look for a domain name that people can spell, remember that you may be reading it out to them over the phone, not just using it in your printed publications or online. Try where you can to avoid hyphens or spaces to make it as easy as possible for people to enter your domain name in their browser.

Don't carry out your searches until you are in a position to buy, as there are domain name snipers who will see the searches you have carried out and buy the domain name if you don't, in the hope they can sell it on to you at a higher price at a later date.

It's also worth considering buying the .com as well as the .co.uk version.

With .co.uk domains costing as little as £7 for two years there is no excuse for using a hotmail or Gmail email address. Use Google Apps free and all it costs is the price of the domain name. It's much more professional and portrays the correct business image.

http://www.123-reg.co.uk

Dreamstime

This photo stock site is a great resource for any blogger. There are a wealth of free images on there, you just need to make sure the relevant credits are displayed alongside the image.

Like most photo stock sites you can pre-buy credits for the paid images (the more you buy the cheaper it is) and just use them as and when needed.

They have a wide range of images available, sometimes I am spoilt for choice! Just remember to check the licence when you buy, you need an extended licence if you are going to be using the image in print. Dreamstime have help and support on the site to advise on this.

http://www.dreamstime.com

Dropbox

Dropbox is a file sharing service that allows you to store and share files and folders on the web for collaborating with clients. It works in the background, syncing files over the internet, and allows you to log in and access files from any computer with an internet connection using your secure user name and password.

Dropbox can be used as a form of backup, especially if you pay a little extra for the ability to restore deleted files.

You can have a mixture of shared and unshared folders in Dropbox. When working with a new client I create a Dropbox folder in their company name and share this with them. I then have sub-folders within their company folder where I can sub-divide the information. This is particularly useful as it means we can both access important information even if the other party is offline. I use this a lot when working with images and website content for clients. It is also an efficient way of sharing large files that would not fit into an email.

Dropbox is available in mobile applications which means that I can access the information from my phone, tablet, netbook, laptop or indeed any machine with an internet connection. Even if I am out and about I can share files and information with clients, which I couldn't do if they were only stored on one machine.

http://www.dropbox.com

Eventbrite

Eventbrite is a ticket sales website that helps you when you are organising events. You can also create tickets for free events. We use Eventbrite for our free intelligentVA coffee mornings, as it allows us to generate a list of people attending the event. There's no charge for using the service if you are giving away the tickets free, and if you are charging for tickets you only pay a % of the ticket price.

Eventbrite allows you to offer discount codes, copy events, show location maps, and even advertise your event to other Eventbrite users or share your event via social media sites. Your event can remain private or invitation only if preferred.

MailChimp integration will allow you to communicate with your attendees before and after the event. Perfect for sending out invitations, pre-course information or course follow-ups.

You can create a physical ticket if attendees need to show one to gain entry, and use their free Smartphone app to scan these tickets to speed up the booking in process.

http://www.eventbrite.com

Evernote

Evernote is one of the best apps I have come across. I have been known to describe it as 'a filing cabinet on steroids', that is available on your phone, tablet or PC.

Notebooks and Notes
You can have multiple notebooks, with notes within each notebook; imagine a whole room full of post it notes all compressed into your phone.

I create a fresh notebook for each client. Think of this as the filing cabinet drawer. Then within that notebook I store individual notes, which can be text, screen clips or audio clips, which relate to that client.

You can share individual notebooks with your clients or associates if you wish or just keep them all private.

Mobile
Evernote is available on several mobile platforms, as well as PC and Mac. It syncs the information between your devices (it's protected by your user name and password being required to sign in and an additional four digit password on your phone if required).

Screen Clips
Evernote is the best screen clipper I have found. I use the short code keys to generate a screen capture and can then specify exactly which part of the screen I wish to save. This clip is automatically saved as a new note. You can now open the image in your image editor and save it in the relevant image format and location on your computer.

Voice Memos
Evernote allows voice memos. Perfect for those who wake up in the middle of the night with the next great idea and don't have a pen and paper to hand but do have their phone on the bedside table.

Account Levels
The free account is excellent, but sign up for premium if you want your notes to sync when you are offline between devices.

www.evernote.com

Express Scribe

This is a great piece of free software if you want to offer transcription as a service.

Simply open the audio file and transcribe. Playback is controlled either by a transcription foot pedal or assigned 'hotkeys' on your keyboard.

You can control the playback speed, and can pause, rewind, fast forward as required.

The free version works on wav, mp3, wma, aif and dct formats, and you can upgrade to play back dss, ds2 and mvf formats if required.

http://www.nch.com.au/scribe/index.html

Facebook

Facebook is not just about catching up with friends from school. Keep your personal and business contacts separate by having your own Facebook business page. You can update your Facebook business page with the RSS feed from your blog, invite people to events, share discussions and offer promotions exclusively to Facebook fans if you like.

There are three main areas to Facebook you need to consider.

Personal
My advice is to keep this personal. This should be for friends and family. If you start to allow business contacts on your personal profile you will always have to think before you type. Do you want your business contacts to know what you were up to at the weekend, do you want to always have to portray a professional image even when talking to family and friends and do you want photos of your children or social life to be seen by people outside your circle of family and friends?

Fan Page
This is where your business should be. This effectively advertises your business, and depending on the type of business you run, can show information such as your opening hours and location. The feed from your blog can be imported, creating fresh content for the page whenever you update the blog. Post comments on the 'wall' to encourage conversation with your potential client base. It's worth remembering that you no longer need the minimum 25 likes to get a unique URL (short Facebook address for your page) so you can advertise your own 'Facebook Page' within your email signature, on your business card, your website or even on your YouTube video! For example our Facebook page address is:

http://www.facebook.com/intelligentVA

Create your own custom welcome or offer pages which match the branding from your website.

Facebook Group

These are really useful where there are a like minded group of individuals who wish to converse with each other. We have an intelligentVA Facebook group which is a closed group. This means that only people who are members of the group can see the conversation, and that entry to the group is moderated. This way Virtual Assistants who are members of the group can discuss confidential information that they would not wish to appear on their Facebook timeline. You can share links, images and posts in the same way that you can on our personal or fan page.

Groups can also be open groups, this means that anyone can join and see the conversation. You just need to decide at the outset who you would like to access the information in your group.

http://www.facebook.com

http://www.facebook.com/intelligentVA

http://www.facebook.com/groups/intelligentva

Feedly

Feedly is a free newsreader and brings together into one place the content that you want to read. It's a great way of following multiple blogs, catching up on the news and suggests other content that you may find of interest.

It takes the content that you have asked for and brings it to you in a magazine style format.

With its Social Media integration you can share this content on Facebook, Twitter and more, enabling you to populate your social media sites with information your followers will find of interest.

Feedly is accessible via your Smartphone, iPad or Android tablet making it easy to keep up to date whilst on the move.

Don't worry if you already use Google Reader, it takes your existing feed and imports it into Feedly.

You can save content to read at a later date, or link through to the relevant website for more information.

It takes a little time to set it up to get the content that you really want, but it's a great way to keep on top of the news in your area of interest, and has meant that I have been able to read some great content I would otherwise have missed.

http://www.feedly.com

FreeIndex

When I first started doing the research for my VA business I found that FreeIndex kept appearing near the top of the internet search results. If you're wanting to work with local clients then you need to be listed on here.

As the name suggests there is no cost involved.

Potential clients can go on FreeIndex and request quotes for a particular project, you receive an email notification to let you know the request is there and can then submit your quotation, it works!

FreeIndex allows clients to leave you feedback, although I personally prefer to receive recommendations via my LinkedIn account. You can add a widget to your website to display this feedback if you wish.

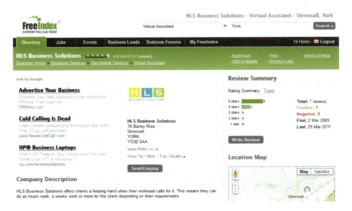

There are other free directory sites that you can list on, you should look at adding your business to Facebook and Google Places as well. Let's face it the more places you can be found the more chance you have of showing up in the right place when potential clients search for you.

http://www.freeindex.co.uk

GetClicky

GetClicky is a really useful website analytic tool.

What we like about it is that it shows you the live traffic on your website, no waiting till the following day to see how many visitors you have had, and shows you how many visitors are on your site right now. Also available as an iPhone app or iPad app, you can keep track of your traffic on the move, and with a simple WordPress plug-in (Clicky by Yoast) it is easy to add to your WordPress website.

The summary screen shows you the number of visitors, which pages they have visited, the total time they have spent on your site, and the bounce rate.

You can also see which sites have sent you traffic, which page visitors are landing on, which page visitors are leaving on, as well as what search engine phrases have been used to find your website.

You can set notifications on the apps to let you know when a certain number of visitors have arrived.

All of the information shown above allows you to access more detailed information, and as I already mentioned, the information is live. It's a great feeling when you post a link to your latest blog post on Twitter or Facebook, open the app and see the visitors online steadily increase.

The free plan allows you to track one website, and there are paid plans available which allow you to track from 3 to 30 sites.

http://getclicky.com/

Google Apps

You may have a Googlemail account but did you know you can get a free Google Apps account? This allows you to have your emails linked to your domain name, share access to documents online, and even share calendars.

Gmail
I moved away from Outlook at the beginning of 2011 because I was tired of losing information when I changed pc and couldn't remember how to restore the backup file, or the pc crashed and refused to restore Outlook, but mainly because I wanted to access my email from wherever I was and for it to look the same and be the same. In other words if I hit delete on my phone I wanted it to delete on my laptop as well. I wanted one list of contacts, I wanted to be able to use my phone, netbook, tablet or laptop or even a friends computer if I was away from the office. I'm not greedy, I just like to stay connected. Google allows me to do this. To start with I couldn't quite give up my Outlook folders so used the Outlook/Google sync tool that linked my email and calendar, but once I understood the 'labels' in Google there was no excuse not to make the move permanently.

My email now filters itself as it arrives, email relating to client A goes into a folder specifically for client A, newsletters go into a folder to be read later when I have time, certain senders go into an 'Urgent' folder, and there's even a filter for my daughter's school who now use email to communicate with me.

Calendar
Google calendar is an excellent tool if you wish to work virtually as you can allow access to other users, they can either view your calendar or view and edit. This means that as a Virtual Assistant you can book meetings on your clients behalf and they automatically appear in your clients calendar.

Another useful feature of Google Calendar is the reminder service. You can choose when you wish to have a reminder arrive and in what format. This means that you can not only book an appointment on behalf of your client but you can set a reminder to go to their mobile phone several hours before as well, other options include pop up or email reminders.

Google Docs
If you have a document that both you and your client need to edit then Google Docs is an excellent idea, it allows for word and excel, albeit without a lot of the pretty formatting, and the best part of it is that you can both edit the document at the same time. It is kind of spooky the first few times that you do this but is so much better than trying to share a document via email, with different revisions. This way there is one document and all the changes are made on the one document.

http://www.google.com/apps/

Health

Okay, I guess you're wondering why Health would be a tool for a Virtual Assistant. It's simple, unless you take care of your health you won't be able to work on your business, so it's a no brainer that you have to take care of yourself.

I've been there, I know the temptation when you are starting out is to work all the hours and forego your 'me' time. Don't do it. All work and no play makes Jill a sick girl. Okay, I admit took some poetic licence there to make that fit but the message itself is a serious one.

You must allow some time for you, some 'me' time. Plan it in your diary now.

It's too easy to get caught in the trap, especially if you work from home, of trying to do it all. Trust me, you will probably find you work more hours now you're self employed than you ever did when you worked for someone else, so you've suddenly increased your hours but all the old demands on your time are still there, the housework, the kids, your friends, the gym and so on. Do you really want to have to give them up?

The other thing to consider is if you get ill how will you pay the bills? The first thing I did when I went full time in my business was to contact my Financial Adviser and take out income insurance. God forbid I should get seriously ill but I would still be able to pay my mortgage. (Contact me if you need an introduction, he does a very good job).

'Me' time can be anything, but it should be something outside of your business; a day out with friends, meeting up for coffee for an hour, a gym session, golf game, visit to the hairdresser or go for a run are just a few suggestions.

It's a good idea if you work from home to set specific times for work; leave your desk at mealtimes, and if possible go out for a walk, just to get a change of scene and some fresh air.

If you do get sick, don't try and work through it, from experience it just drags it out and takes longer to get better. Keep in touch with your clients, let them know what the situation is, and consider having other VAs you can call on should this type of situation arise. Do take the odd duvet day if you need it, remember, your VA business is dependent on you, you take good care of the resources you use in your business, the most important of which is you.

Hootsuite

Hootsuite is definitely our preferred Twitter client on the pc and iPad. It allows multiple Twitter account access, as well as delegation of accounts to members of your team. The interface is clear and simple to use and also allows updates to LinkedIn, Facebook Profile, Facebook Page, Facebook Group, Foursquare, Ping.fm, WordPress and MySpace through the one interface.

Columns
Hootsuite is a column based Twitter client, you can have columns showing side by side displaying your main Twitter feed, your mentions, your direct messages (DM's) and even see which of your tweets have been re-tweeted. You can also set up feeds based on your searches or lists.

Scheduling
When you tweet in Hootsuite you can choose to send the message then and there or to send it later, this is called scheduling. Hootsuite will also allow you to bulk schedule your updates but remember that Twitter will not allow duplicate content so you would need to amend each one slightly in the downloadable spreadsheet before uploading your schedule.

Team Members
You can have team members on Hootsuite, this means that other people can help you manage your account, and you can assign tasks to the team members. You can also see when a team member has responded to a tweet from your account.

Reporting
You can create reports from within the Analytics tabs to monitor your Twitter performance. You can create your own reports or use the pre-built ones. They show such things as how many clicks there have been on the links you have posted. This is useful when you are trying to work out the best way to get your message across.

http://hootsuite.com

iPad and iPhone

It's hard to decide which of these is the better tool, it's like having my office in my pocket, there's hardly anything I can't access from my iPhone or iPad. Email, Calendar, Contacts and Reminders are part of the default set up, and there are 'apps' for pretty much everything you can think of from Satellite Navigation, updating your WordPress blog or even helping you calculate the VAT element of an invoice or receipt.

iPhone
Obviously this is the more portable of the two and allows you to make calls as well. Don't be deceived by the small screen, I have watched ITV player via the iPhone and also started off with the Kindle app on there before buying my Kindle. I've been able to sit and use Xero on my phone and catch up on invoices and bank transactions whilst sat at a seminar in a quiet break. Many of the subjects covered in this book are available as apps on the iPhone.

iPad
The larger screen really does make a difference, there are some apps that I don't use as it's just as easy to access the sites themselves from within the web browser. I am more likely to use the iPad for things like mind mapping, drawing and watching videos, but don't be deceived by the size. It's a very powerful work tool. I sat and designed the intelligentVA website layout on a mind map on my iPad whilst in a hospital coffee shop one morning.

Applications
Of course there are thousands upon thousands of apps available for both devices, and a lot of them are not work related, but over on the intelligentVA website we have a list of our favourite business related iPhone and iPad applications, it's updated as we come across new and interesting apps, and we don't add them unless we have tried and tested them ourselves.

Of course there are other tablets and Smartphone's available on the market, I can only comment on the ones that I use, and confess to being addicted to both of these gadgets.

Information Commissioner's Office

If you are handling data on behalf of a client then you need to register with the Information Commissioner's Office every year. I was struggling to work out my classification when I started out so rang them up, they are amazingly helpful.

They asked if I was likely to advise clients or be involved in the decision on what to do with the data we were handling, and I suspect that this would be something that every Virtual Assistant will do as part of their service. You will also be handling your own data.

Their website states that:

> The Data Protection Act 1998 requires every data controller who is processing personal information in an automated form to notify, unless they are exempt. Failure to notify is a criminal offence. Register entries have to be renewed annually. If you are required to notify but don't renew your registration, you are committing a criminal offence.

If you cannot figure out the correct online classification for your business then ring them up and they will guide you through the process.

http://www.ico.gov.uk/for_organisations/data_protection/notification/notify.aspx

Jing

Jing is a way of recording a video of what is happening on your screen (known as a screencast), and sending it to your clients. It's a much quicker method than writing long word documents with screenshots in there and clients like the simplicity of Jing. There's even a free account. You can specify which part of the screen you want to share in your recording so that you don't have to close other windows down.

Jing sits out of site at the top of your screen until you are ready to use it.

You can use it to capture screenshots, mark them up and then share them on Screencast.com, Flickr, Twitter or Facebook.

The screencast can also be shared on Screencast.com, Twitter, Facebook. Jing can record your commentary at the same time via your microphone.

The free version allows you to record up to 5 minutes of video. The premium version allows Webcam recording, MPEG-4 videos and instant sharing to YouTube.

http://www.techsmith.com/jing/

JotForm

JotForm is a WYSIWYG form builder. I have used JotForm to create order forms, time sheets, competition entry forms, and surveys. You can receive the submission via email or view the results in a spreadsheet format, which is something that other free survey suppliers don't offer as far as I am aware.

It has a drag and drop interface to make it easy to build branded forms, with everything from drop downs, tick boxes and PayPal integration so you can use it to create order forms as well.

You can integrate the forms into your website, post them on Facebook or email a link to them.

What I really like about JotForm is that if I make a change on the form it's instantly updated everywhere without me having to update the website, Facebook or the link I had already emailed.

You have the option to have files to be attached to the form when it is being submitted.

JotForm offers both a free service and a premium service. The free service is feature packed and currently sufficient for all my needs, although I will be happy to upgrade to premium when I need to.

http://www.jotform.com/

Kindle

Kindle is one of my favourite gadgets, don't get me wrong, I really love books, there's nothing better than curling up on the sofa with a good book but I find it much easier to read on the Kindle.

Amazon have a wealth of Kindle titles available, and they're not just fiction. You can read Kindle books on your Smartphone, your PC, your Kindle reader or your iPad or tablet. You don't have to purchase a Kindle itself.

There are some excellent business books available on the Kindle, and because it's so easy to read, you can keep up to date wherever you are. There's also the added bonus that your other half doesn't notice you're reading your business books outside of working hours!

I am a great advocate for continual learning, learning things that are going to have an impact on your business rather than just add fancy letters after your name, and the Kindle gives you that opportunity.

Be it sat on the bus on the way to a meeting, during your coffee or lunch break, or relaxing after work, there's always time to catch up on reading. Check out the Kindle today and you'll probably never regret it.

http://www.amazon.co.uk

Klout

Klout is a light hearted way of measuring the effectiveness of your Social Media activity. It shouldn't be taken too seriously but will show you what it thinks your online networking style is, and how much influence you have among your social circle.

It likes to show you who it believes you are influenced by and who you influence, as well as the topics you cover most. As I said, it shouldn't be taken too seriously but it can show you if your online activity is promoting the message you believed you were portraying or if you need to tweak it slightly.

http://www.klout.com

LinkedIn

If your client market is the professional sector then you need to have a presence on LinkedIn, it's more than just an address book, there is a huge amount of support on there if you join the right groups, and the Question and Answer section allows you to share your experience and build your reputation by answering questions. It is much more formal in tone than Facebook or Twitter.

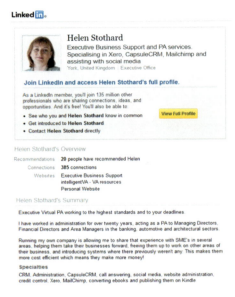

Make sure that you maximise your 'professional headline' (which appears under your name), don't just put owner. This is shown whenever you post in a group on LinkedIn, so encourages people to look at your profile, and potentially connect with you. As you can see from the image above I have listed several of the systems that I work with, making it clear to prospective clients exactly what I offer.

Don't forget to connect with your clients as LinkedIn allows you to ask for and receive recommendations. I prefer to show my recommendations on LinkedIn rather than other systems, as LinkedIn is a very professional network, and adds authenticity.

Recommendations can only be generated by other LinkedIn users. I confess I do keep forgetting to ask myself, so would suggest you get into the habit of asking for a recommendation as you complete a project. You need to be connected to someone before you can ask for a recommendation.

LinkedIn Groups

LinkedIn groups allow you to connect and have conversations with other like minded individuals.

We have an intelligentVA group on LinkedIn where we can discuss issues relating to our Virtual Assistant businesses and get support from other VAs around the world.

http://www.linkedin.com

http://www.linkedin.com/groups/intelligentVA-3906866

MailChimp

MailChimp is an automated email management system, which is often used for newsletters. At the time of writing it is free for up to 2,000 subscribers and 12,000 individual emails per month.

The templates are easy to set up. MailChimp will try to match the colour and feel of your website. There are a large number of templates and layouts to choose from.

MailChimp uses a double opt in system to prevent spam, this means that when a new subscriber signs up to your list (they supply the code for your website and there are several WordPress plug-ins available) they have to click on a link in the welcome email to confirm their subscription, ensuring that only the people who want to receive your newsletter actually receive it, and helping you avoid sending unsolicited marketing material.

You can have multiple lists, each with their own branding, so it's a very effective tool. As you can see from the image above you can even design your own sign up form.

MailChimp is not just for newsletters. You can use the auto responder option to send out an e-course, use different templates to notify your subscribers of upcoming events or special offers, or send to just a fraction of the subscribed list rather than everyone.

MailChimp offers reporting; you can tell who opened your message and if/when they have clicked on your links. It also shows you the industry average for comparison.

There is an iPhone app which allows you to view your subscriber list and reports, and MailChimp offers integration with Twitter, Facebook, a two way integration with Capsule CRM and has integration available with several other applications.

http://www.mailchimp.com

MinuteDock

This is my favourite time tracking software. MinuteDock allows you to share the time information logged with your clients. Logging time is as simple as clicking a button, it has a very simple log bar for adding in the client and task information.

Because MinuteDock is web based it doesn't matter which machine you log on from, your history is always there. Enter the client name prefixed by @ in the log bar and a description of the work carried out (this can be added later), then to start tracking time just click on the timer icon next to the log button. When you've finished click on the timer icon again to switch it off.

You can set goals so you can work towards a specific target; I have one for the number of hours I need to work each week before I can take time off for a coffee meeting with friends, I also have a goal to ensure that I don't go over the agreed number of hours on a particular project.

You can add team members on MinuteDock, so it's an excellent resource if you are working with associates; any time they have worked is automatically added to the invoice information and time tracking.

You can run reports to see which users have logged time by day, week, month or specific date.

You can send an invoice direct to the client via email from within MinuteDock, or if you have the Xero integration, it will send a draft invoice to Xero for you.

It's the simplest system I have come across and has been the most effective for me.

http://minutedock.com/

Mirror.me

This is a recent find that I came across after reading Nikki Pilkington's 30 Day Twitter Challenge. If you use Twitter then Mirror.me shows you your word and tag cloud from the tweets that you have posted.

It's always good to keep an eye on what the internet thinks you are saying in comparison to what you think you are saying.

As you can see my Mirror.me cloud is shown above. The bolder the word the more I tweet on that subject.

Have a look at your cloud, does it portray you the way you want to be portrayed? I'm happy that my cloud isn't just business, it's a balance between professional and family.

Click on one of the words shown in your word cloud and it will suggest people for you to follow who care about the same subject.

http://www.mirror.me

Nefsis

Having tried many webinar tools Nefsis is the best one I have found, it's not the cheapest but they do offer a free account for one to one webinars, which allows video conferencing and does not require a separate audio dial in. It's also very good for screen sharing, particularly when you need to share documents.

At the time of writing the only downside with Nefsis is that they do not support the Mac operating system. There is a workaround available from Nefsis support if your client has a Mac that utilises the Windows environment, but this can be an issue if your client is pretty creative and a Mac user without a Windows environment.

http://www.nefsis.com

Networking

Many Virtual Assistants hear the word networking and start shaking. It's a bit like Marmite in that you either love it or hate it.

Networking shouldn't be something to be scared of, it should actually bring you business if done the right way.

Networking isn't just about turning up at events though. There are other ways to network until you feel ready to meet people face to face.

When I started out I was working a full time job and running my VA business 5 to 9 and then some. I didn't have time to attend meetings, but I found a lot of support networking online.

This can be through social media, such as Twitter, Facebook, LinkedIn or Google+, or it can just be via online forums.

I started out on forums as at that point it was all I knew. There were people like me wanting to make the move to full time self employment, and there were people who were already working for themselves full time. They gave good advice and helped me build my confidence, even introducing me to the social media forms of networking.

> *"Whether you choose physical or online networking the important thing is not to sell, sell, sell. That's not what networking is about, it's about building relationships, sharing connections and giving help or advice where you can."* Helen Stothard

Follow that mantra and the work will start to come to you via referral.

When you're looking to start physical networking have a look round for groups that meet your needs, be that the time they meet, or the requirements they place on you for attending, some require you to attend every meeting whilst others allow you to attend as and when you are able.

Office Space

A separate working area is essential if you wish to be truly effective in your work. A dedicated area with desk space, room for your printer, your phone and ideally a door you can shut to keep the rest of the world out, especially when you are on the phone.

You would be surprised how much more productive you are when your office area is geared around you and not around the rest of the household.

You may choose to work from an external office or from home, there are pros and cons for both, and it's up to you which will meet your requirements best. Some people feel they are only productive when working outside the home, although this is an extra overhead that you need to take into account.

If you do need to meet with clients and your office is home based why not suggest a local hotel lounge where you can meet for coffee, and if they also have free wifi you can also work there from your laptop if needed.

The beauty of being a Virtual Assistant is that when required your office can travel with you, as you can see from the image above, we had everything we needed with us at our intelligentVA learning day from video camera to printer, laptop to iPad and even our portable scanner.

The most important thing is to keep your office clutter free, don't be tempted to buy every gadget or bit of stationery from the outset as you may never need them. I bought a box of envelopes when I started, and am still tripping over them years later.

Payroo

Payroo is a free online HMRC accredited payroll solution. This would be used if you were running your VA business as a Limited Company, as you are an employer, or if you offer a payroll service to your clients. Payroo is free to use and only starts to cost when you have over nine employees throughout the course of the year and are doing your End of Year return.

I came across Payroo when I was looking for a payroll solution that catered for CIS (Construction Industry Scheme) for a client. I have since introduced my accountant to it as it is so simple to use.

Payroo allows you to generate payslips and you can allow employees access to their own records allowing them to submit their timesheet online or print copies of their payslip or P60 when required. You can cut down on printing costs and email the payslip to the employee as a PDF file if required.

If you use the CIS element of Payroo you can do online subcontractor verification and submit your monthly CIS return electronically to HMRC.

You can electronically file your End of Year return direct to HMRC from within Payroo.

http://www.payroo.com

PhotoSync

Now technically PhotoSync is an app for the iPad or iPhone, however I am including it because it wirelessly integrates with your PC.

You're trying to add an image from your phone to your blog, Facebook or Twitter and you want to keep it simple? There's nothing easier than PhotoSync.

PhotoSync can also transfer to Dropbox, Facebook, Picasa, Flickr, and a host of other services without having to connect to iTunes, which was previously the only option for transferring images between your devices.

Open the PhotoSync app on your device, select which images you wish to transfer and send – it's as quick as that with the images then appearing in a dedicated folder in 'My Pictures' on your PC.

PhotoSync can either sync all the images from your camera roll or just the ones that you have selected. You can transfer images between your PC, iPhone or iPad.

This app isn't free but only costs a few pounds and has been worth every penny for the ease of use and flexibility.

http://itunes.apple.com/gb/app/photosync-wirelessly-transfers/id415850124?mt=8

Pixlr

Pixlr is a great free online graphics tool. I've used it several times to create graphics for websites. As well as being available online there are Smartphone versions too.

A lot of graphics software programmes are memory heavy and really slow your machine down. The beauty of Pixlr is that its online, so you can save your projects and work on them from any of your machines.

The grabber extensions available for Chrome and Firefox allow you to 'grab' any image in a webpage and open it direct in Pixlr for editing.

I'll be honest, it's not Photoshop, but for many of the day to day graphics requirements that you have it's a great tool. I've used it for taking an existing logo and extending it into a web graphic, for adding text to images and for resizing and cropping.

http://pixlr.com/

PrimoPDF

This free PDF printer is the best one I have come across. It allows you to save in different quality levels, ensuring that your artwork looks as good in the document as when you designed it, yet also allows for compression so the recipient doesn't have to wait ages for the document to load.

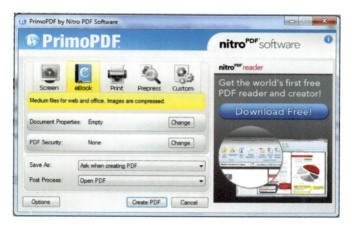

Once installed PrimoPDF shows up in your regular list of printers, just select the option that you require from the pop up screen shown above, and click on 'Create PDF'. You then get to specify the save location on your machine. If you have selected the Post Process of 'Open PDF' you can see how the completed document appears.

PrimoPDF allows you to append pages to a document. Imagine you are preparing a document for a client consisting of Word, PowerPoint, Excel and web pages. You need to print them in the correct order, but you can append to an existing document. This is much simpler than the old method of printing everything off and then scanning it in as one document.

http://www.primoPDF.com/download.aspx

QR Codes

If you haven't heard of a QR code then it's the marketer' best friend. This small square is scannable from smart phones and you can set it for a variety of actions, from getting people to 'like' your Facebook business page, offering them a special discount voucher or even allowing them to save your contact details in .vcf format, all you need is imagination!

You can use SocialQR code to generate Facebook Likes, Twitter followers, share your YouTube content, create discount coupons, and even advertise your Smartphone app.

You can brand your landing page with your own logo or image that will be seen on the mobile page, allowing you to keep your branding consistent.

You can download your QR code as either a JPG or PNG file, or contact the professional printer they use and have your QR codes printed.

This QR code can then be displayed on printed material such as business cards, advertising material or online on your website or Facebook page.

http://www.socialqrcode.com

Rapportive

Rapportive is a download that works in both Firefox and Chrome and gives you information in your Google email box about your contacts, such as their location, position, latest tweets, and links to their social media accounts.

You can see what your contacts look like if they have an image on their social media profiles.

Rapportive takes seconds to install, just use the relevant browser and click on download, your Rapportive will be up and running in no time.

http://www.rapportive.com

SAYNOTO0870.com

This is a brilliant little website for saving money on your phone calls! Check your call tariff with your telecoms provider and many will charge for numbers beginning 08.

Saynoto0870.com is a directory website that allows you to search using the chargeable phone number and brings back a list of results of geographic numbers that will be cheaper to call if not free, depending on your telecoms tariff.

The site isn't the most attractive to look at but when you think about how much money it can save you it will soon become one of your favourite sites to visit!

Simply enter the company name or 08 number in the search box and the site will return a list of alternative numbers for you to use.

http://www.saynoto0870.com/search.php

Skype

Skype allows you to make free video calls or phone calls over the internet and even to share your screen with others. You can also have instant message (IM) conversations either with an individual or as part of a group.

If you are using Skype for business then ensure you complete your profile, using a professional image and selecting what information is available publicly and which information is only visible to your contacts.

Skype groups are an excellent way of staying in touch with several people involved in the same project. Your conversations are stored, meaning you can search back over the conversation at a later date if you have forgotten something that was said.

Skype is one of the tools a Virtual Assistant can use for communicating with clients, be that a scheduled voice or video call to update each other on work progress or a quick question left on IM for them to reply to, when they are back on line.

Skype allows file sharing and it's often overlooked as a method of sharing large files that would block your email account.

You can use the screen sharing function to show your screen with the other person so they can see what you are talking about, and vice versa. Do you really need that face to face meeting, taking you both out of the office, when you could spend the time more effectively on Skype without the travel.

Many of the features on Skype are free to use, but you can buy credit to send SMS messages or make voice calls to landlines or mobiles as well.

http://www.skype.com

SVA – Society of Virtual Assistants

SVA has a special place in my heart as it's the first resource that I came across when setting up my Virtual Assistant business that, not only didn't ask me for money, but showed me that collaboration exists in the VA industry.

Their forum was a refreshing change, people were really sharing help and advice on what did and didn't work, happy to help another VA with product recommendations or just by sharing experience.

Caroline Wylie who heads up SVA is a smart cookie, she has built her own business and really has the respect of the VA industry, she's someone to look up to and admire. I purchased some of Caroline's time not long after my business went full time so she could talk me through her experience of working with associates and it was certainly money well spent.

SVA are also very active in promoting Global VA week in the UK, which normally takes place for a week in May, organising and promoting events throughout the UK and online in a bid to promote the UK VA industry. It's thanks to them that intelligentVA now has regular coffee meetings as they asked people to host them locally around the UK and we enjoyed it so much we carried on meeting every month!

http://www.societyofvirtualassistants.co.uk/

Trainingforvas.com

http://www.trainingforvas.com is the home of the intelligentVA website. I couldn't write an A to Z of Virtual Assistant tools without including this!

intelligentVA is an online resource for PAs and Virtual Assistants, whether they are just starting out or are wanting to take their business to the next level.

The site is crammed full of resources, training, tools and tips to help you move your business forward at a rapid pace.

The site's contributors are all experts in their relevant field, sharing their experience and knowledge. The blog is frequently updated with topics covering everything from starting out to marketing, sales and training opportunities.

intelligentVA has partnered with Sharp End Training to bring interactive training courses to the VA community, enabling learning at a pace that suits you.

http://www.trainingforvas.com

http://sharp-end-training.co.uk/

Twitter

Well it wouldn't be right for me to have an A to Z without my beloved Twitter now would it, after all I am an addict!

I recently spoke to someone just thinking about starting out as a Virtual Assistant and they looked at me in horror when I mentioned Twitter. Do you know what, when I started out, I didn't have a clue what it meant either.

Let me reassure you now, Twitter is nothing to be scared of. Done properly it's actually quite fun as well. The good news is that you can generate business from Twitter.

Twitter is a whole subject on its own, one I have written about in another of my books, How to get started on Twitter and Generate Business.

The thing to remember is that like any other networking activity it's about sharing. Build relationships with people, share ideas and information, show them who you are, after all people buy from people.

Twitter is not only a place for sharing information, you can learn so much on there. I have made some great friends on Twitter, and by reading their blogs and publications have learned so much. I also use Twitter if I am looking for suppliers. I could Google but that just generates a list, I know nothing about the companies on that list. If I ask for recommendations on Twitter then I know that the companies suggested can be trusted, that they can be shortlisted. I've found some excellent suppliers this way and they have never let me down.

There are a lot of VAs on Twitter, follow them and interact with them, remember what we said earlier about collaboration.

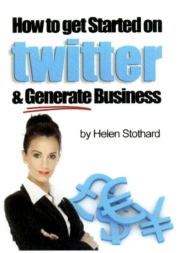

by Helen Stothard

http://www.twitter.com

http://www.twitter.com/intelligentVA

Unlimited Data - mobile

If you have a Smartphone then you need to ensure that you have unlimited data as part of your mobile package, this will allow you to keep on top of your emails, access the apps and cloud software you need via your phone and also allow you to keep on top of your social media statuses as well as accessing the internet. Check the small print on your bill as some mobile providers may say your data is unlimited but still have a level at which they will cap you, or start charging you. If you don't have an internet package on your phone ask your provider if it can be included as an add on or bolt on.

So what uses mobile data on your phone?

Browsing the internet
Cloud Software
Checking your emails
Apps

If possible search for an app for your Smartphone that shows you how much data you are using, there are apps out there that are designed to reduce your data usage but take care that they don't throttle the app you are trying to access in the process.

Another data option to consider is a mobile wireless device. I use the MiFi from 3 Mobile. It allows me to have wireless internet access when I am out and about, and is not a dongle and therefore only of use on devices with a USB port. It's small and portable and will allow me to work on up to five devices at the same time. Perfect if I have the laptop, iPhone and iPad out with me. It's also an excellent back up should your office wireless suddenly go down due to a power cut or failure of your router. They are available on a PAYG or contract basis in the same way your phone is.

My MiFi came in very useful when a client moved office and his telecoms provider let him down for several weeks, I was able to continue working from his business premises.

http://store.three.co.uk

Video

Love it or hate it video is cropping up on more and more websites, I know of one occasion where a VA was hired because she had a video intro on her website.

With the software we have available for free now, there is no reason why you can't create your own short introductory videos, or indeed have video calls with clients, so that working remotely and virtually doesn't mean working anonymously.

- **Website Marketing** – show your customers what you look like, remember people buy from people.
- **Video Conferencing** – some clients are cautious about working with people they haven't met, distance is no object when you can video conference any time you need.
- **Training** – using software such as Jing you can create short training videos for your clients, or with dedicated Webinar software you can run webinars to show several people at once how something works, or hold a discussion.

As well as free software to create and edit your videos there are also apps available on the the iPad to help you with your 'teleprompting', it's certainly a lot easier than trying to balance that sheet of A4 just off camera at eye height!

A lot of people are still cautious about video, I don't even like to have my photo taken so video has not come easily to me. I remember my first client video call, I wouldn't press answer till I had re-applied my lipstick and pulled the brush through my hair, although as time went on I just answered as I was! Make sure you feel comfortable, and if you have your 'battle dress' wear it. The client couldn't see my high heels but they certainly put me in my 'business' frame of mind and made me feel more confident.

And remember, there are lots of applications out there to help you edit your movie, so just keep going until you are happy with the end result then share it everywhere, your website, your YouTube channel, your Facebook page and Twitter.

VoIP

Whilst it may just sound like a jumble of letters to you VoIP could be your best friend when starting up your Virtual Assistant business!

VoIP stands for "Voice over Internet Protocol" – in other words it's an internet phone.

When I started out my VA business I was working full time and running the business on a part time basis. I was running the business from home and not sure if I would be moving to premises when I went full time or not.

I didn't want to advertise a mobile phone number as I think this gives the wrong perception for this type of business, so I purchased a geographic VoIP number. This meant that my business phone had a local dialling code. You can actually purchase a geographic number for any UK area, not just the one where you live.

I started out just adding call credit to the account and diverting all calls through to my mobile, the cost of the divert being covered by the call credit, this meant that the caller didn't know they were being put through to the mobile.

Once my business went full time I invested in a VoIP handset, it looks just like a normal telephone but gives me a business line without tying up the home phone. I don't recommend using the free soft phone option that you can use via your PC as quite often the call quality is very poor.

Your VoIP provider should provide you with a dashboard that will allow you to set office hours, add extensions perhaps or even set diverts at specific times. My VoIP number rings the office phone first then diverts to my call answering team if I am unable to take the call.

There are several VoIP providers out there, shop around and find the one who offers the best deal for you. As with mobile providers they all have different call tariffs and contract/PAYG options so it wouldn't be right for me to suggest one over the other without knowing the type of calls you will be making or the services that you will require.

However, I would suggest looking at Amazon for your handset, you don't have to go for the most expensive model, but do take into account if you're likely to want more than one handset, in hindsight a twin set would have been more suitable for my requirements than the single handset I went for.

The beauty of a VoIP number is that if you do decide to move business premises you don't have to change your phone number or worry that you are now on a different exchange and cannot keep your number, it travels with you wherever you are.

WordPress

WordPress is a free platform that allows you create a free blog or website, and has a host of plug-ins that are available to help you really customise your site. From free themes to custom themes, newsletter sign-up plug-ins to contact forms and Search Engine Optimising (SEO) tools, you can create a website in very little time and also for very little cost as most hosting companies have free one click install of WordPress as part of their control panel.

WordPress is simple to use, easy to upgrade and can be used for blogs, static websites, a mixture of the two and even e-commerce sites or membership sites. If you're not confident enough to do it yourself, then contact us and we can introduce you to WordPress web designers who can create a site for you, and ensuring that it is properly optimised for Google and SEO.

intelligentVA is built on the WordPress platform, as are all my other websites. I love that I can change things as soon as I decide I want them updated, that I can add plug-ins and widgets at will, which mean I don't have to know how to code, and that if I mess it all up I can restore a backup I made earlier.

It's very important that if you use WordPress you keep it updated, I do know of occasions where whole websites have been lost because a hacker gained access via an out of date plug-in. Ensure you back up regularly and especially before you run any updates. Make sure you always have the up to date version of WordPress.

It's worth learning how to look after WordPress, as a lot of your clients will be using the platform and will need your help to keep it up to date and populated.

http://www.WordPress.org

Xero

I once heard a fellow VA describe Xero as *'teaching you bookkeeping by stealth'*.

It's a cloud based accounts system that integrates with MinuteDock time recording, and Capsule CRM to name just a few of the available integrations.

Xero's simple dashboard shows you the latest transactions from your bank account, who owes you money and who you owe money to. Unlike the old accounts systems it's not complicated to learn, and makes the small business owner much more aware of the profitability of their business as well as enabling them to meet their compliance information such as the HMRC VAT Return.

Xero allows you to generate repeat invoices and automatically sends them for you every month, you can edit them before they are sent if for example the amount varies each month, saving you lots of time entering the information.

Xero has the simplest bank reconciliation process I have come across, even allowing you to mark an invoice paid from within the bank. It show's you at a glance what is due in and due out, and highlights overdue invoices.

Xero offer an excellent training and support service for Virtual Assistants, often running webinars especially for us.

Xero just keeps on improving, thanks to their continued investment, and they listen to what we need as the end user.

There are many products which now integrate with Xero, and they can encompass everything from payroll, project management, PayPal, retail tills, and quote production to name just a few.

Xero is one of the few cost options covered in this guide but has been worth every penny. A free trial is available.

http://www.xero.com

YouTube

YouTube - now you have started to create videos for your website why not set up a YouTube channel and share your videos with the rest of the world. It's free marketing for your business and will help enhance your credibility.

There are several plug-ins available on WordPress that will allow you to feed your YouTube channel into your website. You can have the whole channel display, or you can specify individual movies.

Brand your channel so that it reflects your website branding.

Use every opportunity to share your video. Make sure that you include your social media links and website address in the end credits of your video.

http://www.youtube.com

Zemanta

Zemanta is a browser plug-in for Firefox that allows you to add images and links to your WordPress posts by making suggestions as you type the content.

Zemanta is your blogging assistant. It watches as you type and then gives you suggestions for images, content, links, and tags for you to add to your post.

Zemanta updates itself as you type, but you can also refine your search to be more specific. To use an image just click on the suggested images on the right hand side. Zemanta inserts the image for you with the relevant copyright credits.

It takes just seconds to add Zemanta to your browser, but remember it only shows up when you blog in Firefox.

Zemanta will suggest your own previous blog posts for you to include. Once you have used Zemanta for a while on your own blog, your original content will show up as suggested relevant articles to other Zemanta users.

Zemanta isn't only for use on WordPress, it also supports Blogger.com, TypePad, LiveJournal, MovableType, Tumblr, Drupal and Joomla.

http://www.zemanta.com/

About Helen Stothard

I have over twenty years experience of helping business efficiently organise and complete their administration. In 2009, I set up HLS Business Solutions to offer a virtual Executive Business Assistance service to coaches, trainers and consultants.

I am known for my pragmatic outlook and Yorkshire spirit – and am regularly in demand for ideas and inspiration on how to improve administrative processes and implement social media within the business marketing mix.

I am told I am an inspiration to many virtual assistants and people running a 5-9 business. I am one of the few people who have successfully made the jump from a 5-9 business to a 9-5 business. After only six months of running HLS Business Solutions, my proactive service and high standards were so much in demand, that HLS Business Solutions added in four team members – enabling HLS Business solutions to deliver a full virtual executive assistance service.

I am a straight talking northern lass, mother to one, a business owner, coffee drinker, cat food provider, good friend, enthusiastic but slow runner and a twitter addict, not necessarily in that order.

I recently celebrated the second anniversary of making the jump from corporate life to running my own business and I love it. Working from home allows me the time to be mum at the school gate and still get the buzz I need to be me (as well as pay the bills).

Contact Helen Stothard

Helen Stothard
HLS Business Solutions

Tel: 01904 890212

Email:
helen@hlsbs.co.uk

Web and Business Blogs:
http://www.hlsbs.com (HLS Business Solutions)
http://www.trainingforvas.com (intelligentVA)

Skype:
hstothard

Twitter:
http://www.twitter.com/helenstothard

LinkedIn:
http://uk.linkedin.com/in/helenstothard

Facebook:
http://www.facebook.com/hlsbusiness

Personal Blog:
http://www.helenstothard.com

Running Blog:
http://www.runfatgirlrun.co.uk

Printed in Great Britain
by Amazon.co.uk, Ltd.,
Marston Gate.